MW00916148

Safe Travels,
Cheryl

50 Travel Scams You Should Know Before You Go

by C.L. Weekes

What Is A Scam?

"A confidence trick or confidence game, also known as a con, scam, swindle, grift, bunko, flim flam, or scheme, is an attempt to swindle a person or persons (known as the "mark") which involves gaining his or her confidence.

The first known usage of the term "confidence man" was in 1849; it was used by the press during the trial of William Thompson. Thompson chatted with strangers until he asked if they had the confidence to lend him their watches, whereupon he would walk off with the watch; he was captured when a victim recognized him on the street.

Persons of any level of intelligence are potentially vulnerable to deception by experienced con artists.

Just as there is no typical profile for

swindlers, neither is there one for their victims. Virtually anyone can fall prey to fraudulent crimes."

Wickipedia

Table of Contents

"Intellectuals solve problems...

Geniuses prevent problems!"

Albert Einstein

Thieves Are Everywhere

Thieves and con artists may seem more prevalent during your travels because you are the tourist or visitor and out of your comfort zone. Your behavior, attitude, clothing, and/or dialect make you stand out from the crowd no matter how hard you try to blend with the locals. Your best defense from being robbed is to be knowledgeable about your surroundings and not allow yourself to be a willing participant in certain scenarios.

This book is intended to educate and inform you about the most common situations where you could possibly be robbed or harmed. If you are aware of these scenarios before the events happen, you can change the outcomes and enjoy your visit.

Some thieves are fumblers and some are flawless in their craft. One thing they all share in common is that they are always scouting their environment for potential targets. In addition, they are constantly weighing the outcome of a possible action; is the gain worth the risk. In other words, thieves are assessing how much potential money and/or valuables may be obtained from a victim vs. the potential risk of being hurt and/or going to jail if caught in the process of a robbery.

Most thieves are professionals whose only income is that which can be extracted from others – particularly tourists. Many have extensive training in order to perfect their craft. Often children are groomed at a very young age to work for the adult thieves. Training begins by using clothed manikins with bells attached to the pockets. After the children have mastered the art of lifting items from the manikin's pockets without ringing the bells, are they then allowed onto the streets to make money.

There are many scams out there in the world and new ones are constantly being created as the environment dictates. The thieves may be dressed in rags or in riches and can be any size, race, gender, and/or financial appearance. They can be children, elderly, teenagers, middle age, etc. making it very hard to recognize them but you can be knowledgeable about the set-up or scenario in which these people pick their victims.

Awareness and prevention are the keys to a successful journey whether it is for business or pleasure – to a department store or to Spain. This book contains 50 of the most common scams written in three parts: the **Scenario** (what action has just transpired), the **Scam**, (the set-up action taken by the thief), and the **Prevention** (how to avoid becoming a victim).

None of these scam situations were written to frighten or make you paranoid; merely to inform you of the possibilities that you might encounter. Of course, each scenario may appear slightly different during your travels and is intended as a mental trigger when you find yourself in an uncomfortable or potentially dangerous situation.

Familiarize yourself with the information in this book so you can relax and enjoy yourself no matter where your travels may take you.

On
the
Streets

16

Ground Treasures

Someone standing close to you intentionally drops an item of value (money, glasses, tickets, jewelry, etc.) onto the ground beside you. Acting as a concerned citizen, he points to the article on the ground and asks if or states that you dropped it. You looked down and politely say 'no'. At the same time, you instinctively put your hand over your pocket or bag where you are actually carrying your valuables whether they are the same as those valuables on the ground or not.

Scam: The thief has no intention of stealing your valuables then and there.

Instead, he makes a mental note of the exact location where you placed your hand so he or his accomplice can help themselves to your real valuables later.

Prevention: By *carrying your valuables in a secure money belt or zippered pocket in the same location on your person at all times,* you are more than likely not going to have the need to touch your valuables for verification that they are still safe. Thus you are not reacting and providing the information that the thief was searching for.

Uniforms and Razor Blades

You notice a group of young children dressed in uniforms drawing pictures and laughing. They are so cute and notice that they have caught your interest so they gather all around you. They hold out their drawings for you to see. You are honored that they seek your approval so you bend down for a closer look. The children start pushing and shoving each other in order for you to see their picture first.

Scam: While you are preoccupied and distracted with the pictures and the very cute children, you do not feel the little hands that have slid into your pockets or the razor blade that has slit your pocket or bag in order to retrieve items of value.

Prevention: It's sad to think that little children would be a part of this crime, but think about it. Most children (in any country) are taught not to talk with strangers. The uniforms and pictures, as cute as they may be, are simply part of the act. *Do not allow yourself to be surrounded by any group of people (including children) who are close enough to start touching and/or poking you.*

Exchange Rate Plus

A well-dressed man approaches you and in a very articulate manner asks if you would like to exchange money for a rate that is well below the normal exchange rate.

S c a m :
This man has probably been watching you long enough to know that you are carrying a large sum of foreign  currency. He may simply be looking for a way to earn some extra cash but more than likely he has other motives. Although you both are happy with the exchange, the thief now knows how much money you have and where you keep it on your person for a future

encounter where he intends to retrieve it from you one way or another.

Prevention: *Only exchange currency with a reputable business.* Never trust anyone you don't know personally to exchange currency no matter how appealing the rate may be. Just say no thank you and keep walking. Carry enough local currency in your wallet for the day's activities and put the rest of your money in a secure place like a hidden money belt. If you must retrieve more money, do it in a private place away from the view of others.

Angry Faces

You find yourself being surrounded by three or four angry people waving their hands in front of your face and screaming obscenities at you. They start to poke you and pull at your clothing in various places on your body. You are taken complitely off guard, frozen in place and perhaps separated from your traveling companion.

Scam: The main goal of the screamers is not to do physical harm, but to intimidate you and/or separate you from traveling partner. While you are being jabbed and poked, you never feel your bag being opened or pockets being sliced

with a razor blade in order to empty the contents.

Prevention: *Pay attention to your surroundings; walk with confidence.* Notice if a group of people are approaching you and move in another direction. If you find yourself in this situation, start yelling 'stop - thief' or 'police'. Flail your arms and body around and then get away as fast as you can to a safe place.

<u>Strong-Armed Beggars</u>

Walking down a busy street in town, you don't pay much attention to a deformed or crippled beggar sitting on the walkway or curb as you pass by. All of a sudden she grabs your arms, legs, clothes, or bags, etc. Much to your surprise, she is very strong and now you find yourself struggling to be free.

S c a m : Many times these people are not beggars or handicapped in any way. Their intent is to catch you off guard and cause a struggle with you in order to clean your pockets or cause you to drop something of value like shopping bags full of treasures.

Prevention: There seems to be so

much poverty every where we travel that sometimes it becomes a practice to ignore beggars on the streets. **Pay close attention to your environment and the people around you.** Give yourself room to walk around, not next to, someone begging on the curbside if you have no intention of making a donation.

Money Changer

A stranger, who appears to be another tourist like you, approaches you and asks if you have change while displaying a large denominational bill. You pull out your wallet and make change. The stranger thanks you and moves on her way.

Scam: The stranger's intention was to see how much money you had in your possession and where you keep it on your person.  She, or her associate, plans to bump into you at a more convenient crowded place to help herself to your money.

Prevention: *Never make change for anyone you don't know personally.* Politely, but firmly, say

'No' and keep walking away from the stranger. If you feel that you must say something, tell her where the nearest bank is located.

Card Tricks

You stop to watch a street magician perform an act in the park. He is very good and makes everyone laugh. He points to you and asks you to join in the act. Even though you may not speak the local language, you understand and feel honored that he wants you to volunteer for his next act. After he does a few card tricks, he then does another trick by holding up your wallet or watch in plain sight for the crowd to see. You and the crowd clap in amazement.

Scam: You expect the magician to return your belongings but instead he disappears into the crowd. Still clapping, the crowd believes it is just part of his act and does nothing to stop the thief.

Prevention: It's always entertaining to watch a good magician but *never volunteer to be a participant* even if you think it will make a great story to tell everyone when you get back home. Nod your head no and put up your hands in protest. If the magician is still persistent, it may be necessary to leave the area.

Dirty Little Hands

An old woman wrapped in a dirty shawl and ragged clothing begs to sell you a souvenir that she claims she carved herself out of wood or bone in order to feed her children. When you stop to listen to her, she signals her (8) children to come forward and surround you. They all appear dirty with runny noses and bad teeth.

Scam: The children start pressing closer to you crying and pawing for money or food. You never feel their little hands helping themselves to items in your pockets or bags.

Prevention: *Whenever someone approaches you for money or food, firmly say 'No thank you' and keep walking.* If they pursue you, yell for the police. Don't stop to give them a donation or you will be donating a lot more than you intended to. If you feel charitable, there are many local organizations that would gladly accept your donation.

Stickers & Ribbons

A friendly young woman walks up to you smiling and quickly slaps a sticker onto your lapel, or ties a ribbon around your wrist or bag stating that it is in remembrance of your trip. She is carrying a container written with the name of a charity organization. She asks that you make a donation in order to feed all of the homeless children.

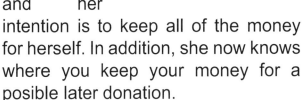

S c a m : There is no legal charity by that name and her intention is to keep all of the money for herself. In addition, she now knows where you keep your money for a posible later donation.

Prevention: If you feel that you want to make a donation, do it through the proper authorities. There are plenty of legitimate organizations that would be delighted to have a donation. *Do not let someone on the street, in the airport, or the bus station tie a ribbon, paste a sticker, or pin a flower on you.*

I Spy Money

You are using an ATM or at a bank window to withdraw money. There are several people waiting in line so as soon as you receive your money you quickly move away to be polite. Still standing close to the line, you count your money, and put it in your wallet or bag before m o v i n g along.

S c a m :

Two things could happen here. As you are counting your money, someone reaches around you, grabs your money/card and runs. Or someone follows you to a more opportune place to steal your money later.

Prevention: *Always   shield*

money transactions with your body. Count your money at the window and put it in a safe place like a zippered inside pocket before turning around. If you are involved in a conversation, speak in very low tones so that others cannot hear or if you don't speak the local language, write the desired amount on a piece of paper and hand it to the teller. Any transaction involving money should be keep as private as possible.

Too Many Drinks

Engaged in a conversation with your traveling partner, you are taken by surprise when out of nowhere a man bumps into you. He smells of alcohol and appears to be intoxicated. His language is very slurred as he apologizes and you notice that he has dropped a personal item.

Scam: The man is actually sober and only pretends to be drunk. As he fumbles and starts to fall as he picks up the dropped item, you naturally reach out to help him. During the encounter, you are distracted as he rummages through your pockets.

Prevention: Pay attention to your surroundings in order to avoid this type of situation. When you see someone who appears to be intoxicated, distant yourself. *Usually when someone bumps into you, you are more than likely being pick-pocketed at that very moment or being set up for the event later.* Keep only a day's or two worth of money in your wallet or bag and the rest of your valuables out of sight and secure with a money belt tucked inside you pants or shirt, or inside hidden zippered pockets.

Conversing in the Park

It's a beautiful day and you feel like taking a break from sightseeing so you go to the park. You spread out your ground cover, sit down, and start writing in your journal or addressing postcards. Someone approaches you and starts to engage you in a conversation. She may say that she wants to improve her English, S p a n i s h, German, etc. and asks you a few q u e s t i o n s. She then asks you

read a passage or two from your writings. Flattered, you let down your guard, enjoy the spotlight and motion her to join you.

Scam: Upon sitting on your cover,

she positions her bag/backpack and sweater next to your belongings. After awhile she says that she has to meet someone. As she starts to gather her bags, she spills some of the contents over your belongings and immediately makes several apologies for her clumsiness. At the same time she is gathering her dropped items she is also gathering some of yours. You do not notice anything missing until she is gone.

Prevention: It is very common for someone to ask to join you. This is a great opportunity to meet the locals but keep your items separated. Put your foot through a strap or drape your leg over your bag. *If someone sits next to your bags, move them to the other side of you.*

A Picture is Worth $1000

Although you used an ATM two days ago, you find yourself running low on cash again. After entering your PIN you discover that you have reached your maximum dollar amount and/or there are no more funds available. You know that there was more than enough money/credit available two days ago but not so today.

Scam: Some thieves use very sophisticate equipment to detect the sound that individual keys make when you push your PIN. Also, it is very easy to obtain your account number and/or PIN by watching you with binoculars, cameras, or camera cell phones. They simply wait until you have left the area or wait until the next day to empty your account.

Prevention: *Cover the ATM keypad* with your other hand or a piece of paper while entering your PIN. Also, *sing and/or talk out loud to mask the keypad sounds.* If you noticed that someone is standing too close to you while using the machine, ask him/her to move back or wait until a less crowded time to use the machine.

Up the Down Escalator

You've been shopping all day in this awesome mall that has multi-levels. You have one more level to explore so you step onto the escalator. For convenience, you rest your packages on the handrail instead of the steps. As you are looking all around at the displays, you suddenly feel your packages being ripped from your hand.

Scam: It is quite common to have the up and down escalators situated side by side in a store or mall. While your head was on a swivel looking at the displays, a thief riding on the opposite escalator saw an opportunity to grab your packages using the element of surprise with very little resistance. He then takes off running the remaining distance on the escalator or tosses the packages to an accomplice on the next level and quickly disappears into the crowd.

Prevention: *Consolidate as many packages into one more manageable package.* While riding the escalator, place your packages on the step that you are standing on or the one in front of you. Use the handrail for what it is intended for – to maintain your balance on a moving object not to hold your packages.

Portrait in Chalk

One of the unique sights of traveling is watching the street artists draw beautiful pictures in chalk on the walkways. As you move in for a better view, the artist asks to draw your picture. He does not wait for an answer and immediately starts drawing you or your companion.

You are delighted but upon completion demands that you pay him. As you try to explain that you did not

ask him to draw you he grabs your arm and pretends that he did not hear or understand you. The more you struggle to free yourself, the tighter his grip and the louder his voice becomes.

Scam: The artist spotted you in the crowd as a tourist and started his act. He knows that you did not ask him to draw you nor were you going to pay him. His intention is to cause a commotion and during the struggle to free yourself, he would pick your pockets. If you actually give him a few dollars to end the encounter, it is a bonus for the artist.

Prevention: *Marvel at the artist's work but do not stand close enough to be grabbed.* When the artist starts to demand payment, walk away immediately without engaging in a conversation.

Mustard Please

Unbeknownst to you, your bag or jacket has something smeared on it such as mustard, ketchup, dirt, etc. A concerned stranger noticing the mess brings it to your attention. At the same time, he pulls out a cloth or handkerchief and proceeds to wipe off the substance. You are very grateful for the assistance, thank the kind person, and move on.

Scam: A thief or his accomplice deliberately smeared something on your clothing or bag. As the "very helpful" stranger's hands are busy cleaning your jacket, he is also cleaning your pockets for any treasures that can be extracted.

Prevention: If someone tells you that something is smeared on your bag, say it's OK and keep walking. *Do not accept the stranger's offer to clean it, instead wait until you are away from the stranger and in a safer environment then clean it yourself.*

This is the number one scam on the streets anywhere in the world.

Cyber Cafes & Wi-Fi Usage

Enjoying one of the wonderful uses of technology while having a steaming cup of coffee has become a common occurrence worldwide. You are one of several customers in the bistro or café receiving and sending emails to all parts of the world in a Cyber Cafe or via a Wi-Fi wireless connection to the Internet. This is also a common event using cell phone with Internet connections.

Scam: Unfortunately, if you are using a Wi-Fi wireless connection without encryption, you have just given the other computer users an open invitation to view all of your files, credit card numbers, passwords, and personal information, etc. stored on your computer. With this method, a thief can sip their favorite latte, get their emails and steal your information while sitting right next to you and no one would know.

Prevention: *Before you leave your office or home test your computer's (or cell phone's) Wi-Fi security system.* Also test the firewall for vulnerable ports and the anti-virus software. While traveling, use a Web-based email when connecting to the Internet at a public hot spot instead of Outlook or Apple Mail. Turn off file sharing and use strong passwords for sensitive files and folders. Consider using an encrypted USB storage device so if you should lose your laptop, you won't lose everything.

While using a public computer, never type anything that you don't want someone else to read. Also, while using the Internet, do not move from site to site. Instead, completely check out of the current site and then shut down the browser. Reopen your browser if desiring to enter the Internet again.

This may seem a bit overcautious but ID theft can make your life miserable and cost you a lot of time and money long after your travels.

Hooked On Bags

Using public toilets in other countries can be an adventure in itself. Upon entering the stall, you hang your bag on the hook positioned on the inside door or you sit your bags down on the floor next to the door to give yourself a little more room. After dropping your pants, you sit or squat down.

Scam: You are shocked to see a hand reach over the door, grab your bag off the hook, and run. Or you see your bags being drugged out from underneath the stall door or the stall wall next to you and disappear.

Prevention: It is always a challenge to use the toilet with bags and/or luggage. *Many toilet stalls have hooks on the back wall of the stalls (use the bottom or inside hook only) or a pull-down shelf to rest small items to help prevent theft.* If you choose to put your bags on the floor, position them next to the toilet and put your legs over them or put your foot through the straps.

Planes
Trains
Buses

Security Blues

For the past 40 minutes you've been inching your way in line to go through security at the airport . Finally, there is only one person in front of you remaining to go through the security machine so you automatically put your belongings onto the table while waiting your turn. The person in front of you proceeds to go through the metal d e t e c t o r arches and sets off  the alarm. He is sent back in line to take off his belt and steps through the machine again only to set off the alarm a second time. Meanwhile another security officer has pushed your belongings onto the conveyor belt that passes through the security-screening machine to the other side where you can no longer see them. This time the person in front of you empties his pockets and successfully goes through the machine. Finally you go through the metal detector arches to discover that your bags are no longer on the table – they are gone.

Scam: You were pre-selected out of the crowd of passengers to steal your belongings before you got into the security line. These thieves work in tandem. They purchase full fare refundable airline tickets that allow them to go through security. One person positions himself several passengers ahead of you and the other falls in line directly in front of you. The whole scene going through the metal detector is staged so that your attention is diverted while the first thief picks up your bags unnoticed, walks around the security area and then exits the concourse.

Prevention: *Never let your bags or items in the plastic bins go through the screening machine until the person in front of you has cleared the metal detector* and the security officer has given you the signal to step through the arches. Sometimes security personnel can be quite insistent on pushing your bags through the machine ahead of you. Stand your ground - the security officers are very aware of this scam.

Make sure that you do not have any objects on your person that would set off the machine so that you may pass through the first time without an incident and be available to retrieve your bags as soon as they roll down the conveyor belt.

Have Coat Will Travel

You have a long wait until your next flight so you decide to do some paper work. In the boarding area you find a couple of empty seats together, place your bags on the floor, take out your computer, and spread out your paperwork. You are so deeply engrossed

in your project that you didn't notice a woman seating herself two chairs down from you. She places her coat over the chairs between the two of you and pulls out her computer as well. Upon noticing each other, she smiles politely and then you both focus back to your own tasks. After a couple of hours it is time to pack up. That's when you notice one of your bags is gone and so is the woman.

Scam: The woman purposely places her coat on the chair between the two of you. While you were concentrating on your project at hand, she picked up her coat to get a tissue out of the pocket. She then laid her coat the bag that she placed next to one of your bags on the floor. Without you noticing, she gathered her belongings, picked up her coat along with both bags and left the boarding area.

Prevention: *Place you bags next to your legs* even if you are using more than one seat. Or put your feet on them or through the straps so that when you are preoccupied with a project, you will be alarmed if your bags are moved.

Missing a Day Later

While riding on public transportation (bus, train, plane, boat, etc.) you sit next to a very nice person and strike up a conversation. You feel that this person is trustworthy so you leave your bags on or under your seat while you use the rest room. When you return, it appears that none of your belongings have been touched. You continue to enjoy the rest of the journey and conversation until one of you departs.

Scam: While you were away from your seat, it was an open invitation for your seat companion to rummage through your bags. Although it appeared that nothing had been touched, the thief has removed a credit card, phone card, one or two checks, passport, or jewelry, etc from your belongings that will not be discovered until after you or your seat companion has departed.

Prevention: *Never leave anything of value unattended no matter where you are – take them with you*. If you must leave them while you are away, secure the zipper and handles with a cable or lock.

Drugs and Customs

You have just gotten off a long flight and now you have a three-hour layover until you next flight. After sitting in the boarding area for a while, you need to use the toilet. An honest-looking person is standing next to the rest room entrance with several bags next to him. He says that his wife has a touch of food poisoning or diarrhea and will be using the facilities for a while. He tells you that if you want to leave your bags next to theirs he will watch them for you so you don't have to hassle with them while using the toilet.

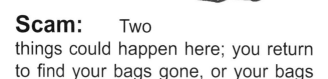

Scam: Two things could happen here; you return to find your bags gone, or your bags are still there, you thank the person and move on. Unbeknownst to you, the man has planted contraband in your bags to be picked up by an associate after you go through customs. If you get caught, it is you, not the 'honest-looking person', who will have to deal with the authorities. If you clear customs you will be followed until there is a more opportune time and place to retrieve the contraband, possibly putting you or your family in harms way.

Prevention: *Never leave your bags unattended or with a stranger.* Take them with you no matter where you go. If your luggage becomes too much of a hassle, perhaps you it would be better to take fewer bags.

35,000 Foot Disappearance

Your plane has just reached cruising altitude and you begin to relax on your flight. You pull out your laptop, notebook, iPod, PDA, or cell phone, etc. from you carry-on bag. After a while you need to use the rest room and stretch your legs. You leave your item on your seat and return a few minutes later to discover that it is gone. You report this to the flight attendant and ask the passengers seated around you if they saw anything but they all answer no.

Scam: Most passengers are engrossed in their own thoughts or actions and not paying any attention to the other people around them let alone your items left in the seat. But one passenger is paying attention and as soon as you are gone, they walk by, pick up your item and walk to their own seat unnoticed.

Prevention: *Do not assume that you are safe from theft because you are in a tube suspended at 35,000 feet in the air.* Take your valuables with you or secure them to the seat leg in front of your seat with a cable lock running through the zipper. There has never been a flight delayed or emergency landing in order to search the plane along with its passengers for a stolen laptop no matter how sensitive the stored information is.

"The rewards of the journey far outweigh the risk of leaving the harbor."
Unknown

Lodging

Lobby Ambience

Hotel/motel lobbies are public places where many people enjoy the ambience by reading the paper or book, sipping on a beverage, or talking on the phone, etc. When you step into the lobby and look around, you feel the safe and enjoy the ambience as well. You notice an open space next to a huge potted plant so you park you luggage there and then proceed to check in at the front desk. Within a few minutes, you have your room key in your hand and turn to retrieve your luggage only to see that there is nothing next to the plant.

Scam: Since hotel/motel lobbies are public places, many people who enjoy the ambience are not hotel guests. Unattended luggage is an invitation for someone, other than the owner; to walk out the door with him or her and no one would be suspicious.

Prevention: *Keep your bags with you at all times or pay a porter to handle them for you.*

Knock-Knock

There is a knock on your hotel door. You open it to find a man dressed in clean overalls with the hotel's name and logo embroidered on the collar. He states that he is supposed to fix the heating/cooling system or fire alarms, etc. so you let him in. He opens his tool bag and starts disassembling the equipment. After a few minutes, he says that this might take  awhile and suggests that you go to the lobby for a soda where you will be more comfortable while he fixes the problem.

Scam: Actually he does not work

for the hotel. It is very easy for people to acquire work clothing that hotel employees wear. As soon as you leave the room, he is filling his tool bag with your belongings and walks out of the hotel unnoticed.

Prevention: *Never open your door to anyone without calling the front desk* to verify the situation first no matter how official they may look and/or present themselves. Do not speak to the person through the door either - promptly call security if there is no response with the front desk. If the person at the door is indeed a thief, let the hotel security deal with him, not you.

Fingerprints

You are delighted to have a small safe in your hotel room to store your valuables and so you don't have to carry everything on your person while you are sightseeing for the day. You punch in your own code on the keypad, shut the safe door, and off you go feeling confident that your valuables are secure. When you return to your room, you discover the safe door is open and all of the contents are gone.

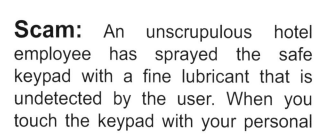

Scam: An unscrupulous hotel employee has sprayed the safe keypad with a fine lubricant that is undetected by the user. When you touch the keypad with your personal code that you have chosen, you leave an impression or fingerprint on those specific keys. When you have vacated the room, all a thief has to do is dust the keypad to determine which keys were touched in order to open and empty the safe.

Prevention: Always test the locking and unlocking mechanism of the safe with your personal code before you store your valuables inside. If the safe or your code does not work properly, report it to the front desk. ***Touch all of the keys on the keypad and/or then wipe them with a clean cloth*** after you have closed the safe. Be sure to do this every time you use the safe.

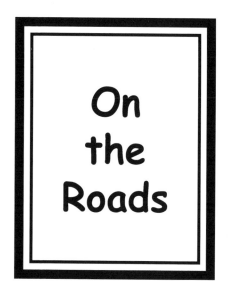

On
the
Roads

Rentals and Luggage

It's been a long flight. There's been one delay after another and you have finally arrived at the auto rental agency. You park your bags next to the windows and get in line. Listening to the screaming children standing in line in front of you is giving you a headache. All you want to do is rent a vehicle and drive directly to the hotel. Finally it's your turn and  now you have the keys in your hands for the rental car. When you leave the counter to retrieve your bags, they are gone.

Scam: Between the screaming children and the rental agreement you never noticed a woman/man stroll out the door with your bags. Thieves are everywhere - even in rental agencies. Some will rent a vehicle just to be in the agency for the sole purpose of stealing an unsuspecting customer's bags. The price of a rental is cheap compared to the treasures they may find in your bags.

Prevention: Many people let their guard down once they are off the plane and forget to keep their bags with them at all times. No mater what part of the journey you are at - *keep your bags with you at all times – even in the auto rental agency.*

The Good Samaritan

You had a great day at the museum and get into the rental car to go back to your hotel. At the intersection you notice someone   frantically waving and pointing to your auto's back tire. Concerned that there is something wrong, you pull to a stop on the side of the road and get out. The observer runs up to meet you   continually speaking very fast and frantically pointing as walk to the opposite backside of the car to look at the problem.

Scam: This scenario requires at least two people. As soon as you walk to the other side of the auto, the second thief jumps into the car and drives away with all of your belongings because you left the keys in the ignition. While you are watching the get away, the other thief disappears as well.

Prevention: *If you suspect that something is wrong with your rental keep driving to a police station, gas station, or crowded area.* By stopping, you could possibly be putting yourself in harms way. It is much cheaper to buy a new tire than a replace your valuables and possibly a new car. Always take the keys out of the ignition when you leave the driver's seat even if you are the only car stopped.

Bumper Cars

Listening to your favorite song on the radio while driving to your next destination, you reach to turn up the volume. Surprised that the auto behind you speeds up and bumps you, you pull into the next lane assuming that the driver will pass ahead of you. Instead, he pulls into the same lane as you and he rams you again. Shocked and suspecting possibly damage, you pull off to the side of the road and get out.

Scam: This is not road rage; this is a common practice with certain thieves. When you to pull off to the side of the road, the thief will position his vehicle in front of yours for a quick departure. As soon as you get out of your car, he intends to rob you and speed off into the traffic.

Prevention: *If you are bumped or rammed while driving an auto, do not pull to the side of the road and get out* whether to assess the damage or confront the other driver. If you have a cell phone, now would be a good time to call the police. Keep driving by constantly changing lanes until you get to a police station or some other crowded area. Write down the offender's auto license and type of vehicle to report it to the authorities.

Baseball Bats and Scooters

In some places, traffic is a constant stop and go process. So you find your self creeping along a four-lane highway at the speed of a snail. In the rear-view mirror, you notice a motor scooter weaving through the traffic and wish you were driving one of those at this moment. All of a sudden there is a c r a s h i n g sound and broken glass  spraying throughout your vehicle.

Scam: Thieves are very creative and use the element of surprise to their benefit. By driving a motor cycle or scooter, they can easily maneuver through heavy traffic. If your auto window is open, they can simply reach in and grab your bag or briefcase and be gone before you can get your seat belt unlatched. If the window is closed, a baseball bat can easily smash open the window to get at the treasures inside.

Prevention: *Do not leave valuables sitting on the car seat in plain view.* If it is not convenient to lock them in the trunk, put them on the floor. Cover them with a jacket (not a road map) or secure the handles to the auto. If you there are more than one of you in the car, have your companion put his/her foot through the handles on the floor.

Wet Paper

The weather has turned a bit nasty. It is rainy and windy so you hurry to get into your car. As you turn on the ignition and start to put the car into gear you realize that there is a flyer placed under the wiper and/or the back window. So you shift gears back into park while leaving the engine running and then you get out of your car to remove the flyer.

Scam: A

thief, not a solicitor, put the flyer on your window. Only a car or two away from your vehicle, he was watching and waiting. At the very moment that you get out of your car to remove the flyer, he uses the element of surprise to push you away from the vehicle or forces you onto the ground and steals your belongings. Or worse, jumps into your car and drives away with your car, identity, hotel key, passport, etc.

Prevention: Always be vigilant even if it is pouring down rain. Lock your doors as soon as you enter the vehicle. *If you notice a flyer on the windshield after you have started the ignition, drive away to a better location to remove it if possible. Or remove it while seated.* Never leave the engine running and be sure to remove the keys.

Flashing Lights

Driving in an unfamiliar location can make you a little anxious. You noticed that the driver behind you just reached out his window and stuck something on the auto's roof. Now you see flashing red lights in the rearview mirror. Since you are a law-obeying driver, you pull the car over to the side of the road followed by what appears to be a police car.  A uniformed officer walks up to your window and asks you to step out of your car and show your identification.

Scam: This person is an imposter. While you are standing on the side of the road, hijackers steal your auto with all of its contents. Or you are force to give the officer all of your money to avoid going to jail.

Prevention: Have the local police number programmed into your cell phone or readily available for this very moment. *Keep driving and call the police to give them the license plate number of the vehicle following you and your location.* Tell the police that you are going to keep driving until you find a more public place to stop and ask for assistance. When you do stop, do not get out of your vehicle until help arrives. If the officer is an impersonator, he will not follow you where there are witnesses.

Flat Rescue

You had a great day looking at all the artifacts in the museum. Exhausted, you walk to your parked vehicle. Just as you start to open the door, you notice that one of the tires is flat. Since this is a rental there may not be tools in the trunk in order to change the tire your self. Just as you are calling the rental agency, a very nice person offers to help with the task. After the job is done, he looks at his watch and makes a comment that this task has taken more time than he had anticipated. He tells you that he is going to be late for his appointment and he parked his car on the other side of this lot. He asks if you wouldn't mind

driving him to his car to save time and of course, you obligingly do.

Scam: The air was intentionally let out of your tire while you were in the museum. Since you are very grateful for the assistance you don't question why this person is on this side of the parking lot when his parked car is on the other side and you happily agree to drive him. Once he is in your car, he is able to rob you or demand that you get out of the vehicle leaving you standing there with nothing.

Prevention: When you notice that you have a flat tire walk back to the museum to *call security and the rental agency.* Do not allow a stranger to change the tire or get into your vehicle and don't try to change the tire yourself.

Run Away Fill-Up

The gas gauge in your vehicle is showing about a quarter of a tank of gas remaining so you pull into the next station. Although you turn off the engine, you leave the keys in the ignition while you get out of the vehicle to fill the tank. For some unknown reason, the gas machine will not accept your credit card or the attendant tells you that you have to go into the building to pay.

Scam: An unlocked car is an open invitation for someone to get into your auto and steal your belongings while you are inside the store. If you are paying for the gasoline after you have filled the tank, the thief has a bonus if his intentions are to steal the auto as well.

Prevention: *Always take the keys out of the ignition any time you get out of the car* even if you are standing right next to it to pump gas your self. Keep all of your valuables locked in the trunk and take your bag with you if you must pay inside a building.

"A traveler without observation is a bird without wings."
Moslih Eddin Saadi

Taxi
Cabs

Trunk Ahoy

After waiting a half an hour for your bags to arrive at baggage claim, you step outside. A taxi driver grabs your bags and puts them into the trunk of his cab before you have an agreement to use his services. He keeps smiling and nodding his head while holding open the rear passenger door and motions you to get in.

S c a m :

The taxi driver is counting on your confusion and the use of his services since he already has your luggage in his trunk. If you protest and demand that he remove your bags from his taxi, he may drive off with your bags. Later he may sell your treasures or follow you to your destination and demand payment from you to return them.

Prevention: *Never let anyone take your luggage without your permission.* Negotiate the destination and payment method before the luggage is put into the trunk and you get into the taxi.

Ticket Robbery

After getting into the taxi, the driver seems very friendly and strikes up a conversation with you. He ascertains the nature of your visit and offers to get you special tickets to an event of interest. He says that he gets them at a huge discount because his cousin works for the company and he is willing to sell them to you at a discount.

Scam: If the tickets are legal, you probably will be paying more than if you bought them through regular means. More than likely, the tickets are fakes. His objective is to see how much money you have on your person and where you keep it as he may be contemplating robbing you.

Prevention: *Politely tell the driver no thank you – that you have already made arrangements for the events*. Some drivers can be very persistent so you may have to repeat this statement more than once.

Trading Rooms

You and the taxi driver have agreed to take you to your hotel so off you go. A couple of blocks down the road the driver asks you again what is the name of your hotel. This time he apologizes for not paying closer attention and informs you that your  hotel is temporarily closed while they are remodeling due to water damage, new carpets, painting, etc. He offers to take you to better hotel at a lower rate. You are grateful for the suggestion and agree to go to the other hotel.

Scam: Your original hotel is in fine operating condition. Although the other hotel may be a better establishment, the driver is paid a commission for every guest he brings. Meanwhile, you are charged for the original hotel room for not canceling your reservation within the allotted time frame as well as the new hotel room.

Prevention: It is always a good practice to *call your hotel prior to your arrival to confirm your reservation.* At that time you would have been informed if there were any problems. If the taxi driver insists upon taking you to the other hotel, tell him that you want to see the damage for your self and if true then he can drive you to the other hotel.

Going Nowhere

The sights and sounds of a long awaited destination can be exciting. Your taxi driver over hears you mention that you want to go sightseeing as soon as you drop off your bags at the hotel. He offers to take you on a private sightseeing outing to show you places that are off-the-beaten-track since he has lived in the area all his life. The fee is very reasonable but he wants you to pay him now so he can get gas and refreshments for the trip. He will take you  to your hotel in order to check in and then pick up everyone in an hour.

Scam: By taking your money in advance, he has no need to return. The only sightseeing you will be doing is from the hotel driveway.

Prevention: *If the driver is sincere about taking you on an outing, he would not ask for money* in advance. He would probably give you his name and phone number in order to contact him after you check in at the hotel and make arrangements for the outing at a later time.

Thrown Out

Having visited this city several times, you are fairly knowledgeable with the roads around the airport area and particularly, to your hotel. About half way to your hotel, you look around and notice that none of the surroundings look familiar. You mention this to the driver and he says that there is a lot of construction on the major road to your hotel. Not to worry because he

knows a short detour and you'll be at the hotel in the same amount of time. All of a sudden, he stops the taxi, gets out, opens the trunk and throws your luggage onto the road. He starts yelling, waving his arms, and pointing while demanding that you get out of the taxi. Shocked, you get out thinking that there might be something wrong with the vehicle. As soon as you are out of the door, he jumps back into the taxi and speeds off. Within minutes another taxi arrives.

He apologizes for the other driver's behavior and offers his service at twice the fare.

Scam: The first taxi driver had no intention of taking you to your hotel. He and the other driver work this scam in tandem. They know that you are now stranded; not knowing the area and you will gladly pay the double fare to return safely to your hotel. So they meet up after you are dropped off at your hotel, split the inflated fare amount and go back to the airport for another customer.

Prevention: Most taxi scammers are counting on the fact that you have not written down any identifying information in order to be able to report it to the police. *Every time you get into a taxi, jot down the time, cab number, and/or driver's ID number.* Most incidences can be avoided if the driver knows that you can identify him. Pay attention to the street names and use your cell phone to call the police if needed.

"Heros take journeys,
confront dragons,
and discover the treasures
of their true selves."
Carol Pearson

Shopping
and
Credit Cards

<u>*Our Shop*</u>

Taxi drivers and tour guides know the best places to eat, sleep, and see in any location. And of course, the best place to shop. They claim that their favorite stores have the best quality and best prices in town so off you go.

Scam: These particular stores are usually not in the tourist sections of town. Although it may be exciting to shop "where the locals shop" – the locals know better than to shop there. These shops usually charge more for their products than the ones in the tourist section and the drivers have agreements with the shop owners to receive a commission for every purchase you make in their

stores. And if you don't purchase something, you may have to find alternate transportation back to your accommodation.

Prevention: *Do your homework* by reading books/magazines, the Internet, consult the local tourist agency, and/or your hotel personnel at your destination *for the best places to shop.*

The Genuine Thing

It's always nice to bring home a souvenir to your loved ones at home or as a remembrance of your trip. Because of the size and weight restrictions, it needs to be small enough to pack in your bag. The store merchant or some children on the street approach you holding the perfect item. They claim it is a genuine artifact – a part of history that you will not find anywhere else. You are thrilled, pay the price, and can't wait to show all of your friends when you return home.

Scam: The souvenir is probably a fake and sold to every other tourist who passes by. Genuine artifacts are illegal to remove or sell in almost every country in the world. If the item is an artifact, the seller's intention may be to sell it with no regard to its value or perhaps smuggle it through customs in your luggage only to have a cohort retrieve it later possibly putting you in harms way.

Prevention: *Never buy items that may appear to be genuine artifacts unless you do it through the proper authorities and declare them in customs.* If caught by the local authorities or customs agent, illegal possession of a genuine artifact may put you in jail without a trial or representation no matter how innocent you are.

Be My Precious

You can truly get some great deals while shopping in other countries, especially for jewelry. The sales clerk notices that you have been admiring some beautiful precious stones. To help close the sale, she tells you that you can sell these stones back home for 100% or more than the purchase price. Or you might be told that the embassy will buy back your gems at 100% profit to you. Additionally, the stones come with a certificate of authenticity.

Scam: Be very wary of claims that sound to good to be true. Any sales clerk that would voice these types of sales pitches is unethical and lies. Embassies do not buy any products or jewelry from tourists and custom agents laugh at the fake stones or certificates of authenticity. Taking them through customs may require you to pay the extra duty on the stones regardless if they are fake or genuine.

Prevention: *Only buy precious and/or semi-precious stones from a reputable store or dealer.* Your hotel personnel can advise you where to shop and what you could expect to pay for quality jewels if you are uncertain. Always show documentation of purchase when declaring any item in customs.

Fresh Produce

It's a thrill to mingle with the local people in a crowded market place. You stop to buy a souvenir or food and set your other purchases on the ground next to you as you pull out your wallet to pay. When you bend down to pick up your packages, they are gone.

S c a m :

Many tourists get so excited b a r t e r i n g with the vendors and shopkeepers that they are not paying  attention to their other purchases. It is so easy for a thief to walk next to you, pick up your packages and disappear into the crowd without anyone noticing

Prevention: *It is always best to combine small packages into one larger bag that is more manageable.* If you must set your packages down, place them between your feet and secure them by pressing your legs together. Or set them between yourself and the counter.

Wrapped in Pretty Paper

It's very obvious that you are delighted to find a very unique item that you know your sister will love to have. The shopkeeper agrees with you and takes the item back to the counter in order to process the sale. She puts the item on the inside ledge of the counter and clumsily pulls out a sheet of pretty paper to wrap it for you and/or fumbles with a bag or box to put it in. When she is finished, she smiles, hands you your item and wishes you and your sister a good day.

Scam: If the shopkeeper is unnecessarily handling your item on the way to the counter, she may be using her body to shield the fact that she is switching items en route without your knowledge. Or while she is fumbling with the paper, bag, or box she has made a switch and wrapped a less valuable item instead. You will not be aware of the switch until you open the package.

Prevention: Take the item to the counter yourself. If the shopkeeper insists on carrying it herself, inspect it again to make sure it is the same item once the shopkeeper has set it down. If the item is placed on the inside counter, *never take your eyes off of it until it is wrapped and in your hands.*

Name Change Cards

Eating in restaurants can be a delightful experience. This was a fabulous meal and you are paying with a credit card. The waiter takes your card to process the transaction while you finish your coffee. When it is returned, you put the card in your wallet, sign the receipt and leave the establishment. The next day you attempt to purchase tour tickets with the same card you used in the restaurant only to be denied credit. Upon inspection of your card, you notice the name on the card is  not yours. When you return to the restaurant, the waiter is gone and no ones anything about your card.

Scam: The waiter processed your

transaction for the dinner and returned to you a card that looks just like yours with a different name on it. Actually, the waiter has several fake credit cards in his possession and made a switch with your card. You automatically took the returned card without looking at it and put it in your wallet. The waiter now has your credit card and signature. And as soon as you leave, he proceeds to use it. By the time you discover the switch and report it to the credit card company, the waiter has maximized your limit.

Prevention: Whenever you use a credit card to make any type of purchase, *always verify that you are returned the same card.* If you encounter a switch, report it to the manager or owner immediately. Also call your credit card company to report the theft and stop the usage immediately.

Slipped Through the Cracks

Standing in a long line to purchase your items is not something you want to do while on your trip but you could not pass on the great sales the store was having. Finally you are at the counter and use your credit card to pay for everything. The friendly clerk hands you the receipt to sign and proceeds to put all of your items in a bag. Smiling, she hands the bag to you and thanks you for shopping at this store. You realize that she has not returned your credit card and ask her to return it. Her response is that she has already given it to you when you signed the receipt. You tell her that she did not but she insists that she give it back to you. She appears to be very annoyed and hands you a piece of paper to write down your name and phone number in case someone finds your card. She proceeds to tell you to move away from the counter so that she can help the next customer.

You check your wallet and pocket one more time but no card. By this time the clerk is getting very angry and raises her voice demanding that you move away from the counter so she can wait on the other customers or she will have security escort you out of the store. by now, the other customers waiting in line are getting very annoyed with you as well.

Scam: As soon as the clerk ran your card through the processor, she dropped it behind the register, slid it out of sight near the counter, or slipped it into her pocket without being noticed. She then handed you the receipt to sign as if nothing had happened. When you asked for your card back, her intention was to argue and embarrass you so that you would leave.

After she closes out her station, she retrieves all of the credit cards that she has confiscated during her shift. Later she is able to charge as many items as the cards allow before they are reported stolen.

Prevention: Do not be intimidated by someone raising their voice at you. ***Remain at the counter*** and in a calm voice, tell the clerk that you are not leaving until you speak to the security personnel and the police. ***Use your cell phone to call the police (just in case the security on duty is part of the scam) even if the security personnel arrives within a few minutes.***

When the authorities arrive, explain the situation and ask them to check behind the register, counter, and/or the clerk's pockets.

Double Take

It is so nice to have a camera to take those once-in-a-lifetime-pictures. Also, it's quite common to see people using their cell phones to take pictures as well. So you didn't pay much attention to the cell phone sitting right next to the counter register when you used your credit card to make a purchase. You signed the receipt and stowed your credit card in its proper location. That night when you were using your card again to purchase theater tickets, your card was denied because you had reached your credit limit.

Scam: You did not notice that the

clerk had taken a picture of the front and back of your credit card. At the end of her shift, she makes a copy of your credit card that contains your account number, signature, and the 3/4-digit security code on the back of the card. Since many credit card purchases are automated and/or very few businesses ask for identification, it is easy for a thief to use your card too.

Prevention: Always pay attention to your surroundings. Be on the alert if you see something suspicious or out of the ordinary *and ask for your card back immediately.* I suggest that you write, "see ID" on the signature line instead of your name. This will not stop automated and Internet purchases but it will deter in-person purchases.

Trash Treasures

Since you have stayed in so many hotels during your travels, you have come to think of them as 'home'. Each night you empty the contents of your wallet and/or pockets onto the top of the dresser and you toss your unwanted receipts from your purchases throughout the day into the trash bin.

Scam: Not all housekeeping personnel are honest. Left alone in your room with no one watching, it is the perfect time for the housekeeper to go through you items laying around, especially in the trash to retrieve credit card numbers and signatures.

Prevention: Do not throw any receipt with a credit card number on it into the trash. Keep it with your valuables until you have another place to dispose of them. It is best to tear the receipts into little pieces and dispose them in separate trash containers. Also, do not leave credit cards and/or valuables lying around your room - take them with you. *No matter how honest you think a person is, do not tempt them by having items easily available.*

Sheep vs Goat

Having custom-made couture clothing is a wonderful luxury especially while visiting another country. You go to the shop and discuss with the tailor what you would like made for you. After you pick out the colors and type of fabrics, your body measurements are taken for a perfect fit. Three days later, you pick up your new custom-fitted clothes. Since you are so delighted with the results, you decide to order a few more items along with a designer Cashmere coat. Once again, you arrive at the shop three days later to pick up your items and all is available except the coat. You are told that they have had a delay in obtaining the Cashmere fabric that you requested and they will ship the coat to you as soon as it is ready, estimating the time to be within the next few weeks. You are also told that you must pay for the coat and the customs duty charges in advance.

Since you have been so pleased with the quality and price of the clothing you have already received and the timely manner in which the shop has delivered your items, you have no reason to doubt the sincerity of this transaction. So you pay for the coat and enjoy the rest of your visit. After waiting a month or two, you get a notice from the post office stating there is a package for you and you owe X amount of money for the duty charges. Although you are a little annoyed at the extra expense, you are so excited to get the coat that you pay the extra charge. After opening the package, you discover that there has been a switch.

Scam: The shop owner had no intentions of shipping you the Cashmere designer coat that you ordered. Instead, he mailed you a wool coat that a previous customer had ordered and rejected for whatever reason. In addition, he mailed the package to you claiming the coat's value to be that of a Cashmere designer coat and you were charged with the extra duty expenses. After discovering the switch, you call the shop owner who denies everything and accuses you of lying. You are now the proud owner of a wool coat, not Cashmere, that is not your size or style. Both you and the tailor know that you will not be returning the coat either.

Prevention: *Always shop in a reputable shop.* It is best to purchase items that can be obtained during your visit time only unless you have done business with this shop before and/or plan to visit that area again in the very near future.

Also, if a duty is to be charged on the shipped items, do not pay the shop owner in advance. It is the destination country that controls the imported duty charges not the shop owner.

Fraud Alert

You receive a phone call from someone stating that he works for your credit card company and there has been a questionable charge against your card. After a brief explanation of the suspicious activity, he states that he needs to verify some of your personal information in order to make sure you are the actual cardholder and asks if you have the card in your possession. Then you are asked to verify the 3 or 4 digit security code number on the back of your card in order to place a fraud alert. From this moment on, you are told not to use your card and a new card will be mailed to you immediately.

Scam: There really has not been any suspicious activity on your card except by the thief that is calling. With the personal information you gave him along with the 3 or 4 digit security code, he is able to use your card. You will not report the illegal activity for several days or weeks since you are waiting for your new card to arrive (which it won't) or until you get the next billing statement, which now shows many new purchases that you did not make.

Prevention: *Reputable credit card companies do not ask for personal information regarding your account over the phone.* Do not continue with the conversation if you should be approached in this manner. Even answering a question with a yes or no could jeopardize your account. If you believe that this is a legitimate situation, ask for the contact person's name and a phone number to call back. Then call the credit card company phone number that is on the back of your credit card to verify the circumstances. If the credit card company suspects foul play, they will usually contact the police on your behalf.

Remember...

Thieves are always on the lookout for targets.

They are looking for clues and accessing
what's in it for them (***gain***)
vs.
possible injury and/or jail time (***risk***)
by means of:

- Watching your body language
- Listening to your conversations
- Assessing your appearance and accessories

The best defense is to:

minimize the **Gain**
and
maximize the **Risk**

- Walk alert and on purpose with your head up

- Look people in the eyes

- Know the norms and mores of the area

- Pay attention to your intuitions

- Do not put yourself in harms way

- Walk in well lit areas

- Be knowledgeable of scams

- Keep personal items out-of-sight and in a safe place

- Let someone know your itinerary

- Seek help if threatened

Keep in mind that the majority of the people you will meet during your travels are honest, hard working individuals. Unfortunately, there are a few deceitful people in this world who give every one else an undeserved, bad reputation. Being prepared to recognize a possible scam scenario before it happens, will allow you to...

Make a Memory

and

Enjoy Yourself

This little book
makes a great gift...
whether the receiver is
going on his/her
first trip or is a
seasoned traveler!

The price of this book
is well worth
"an ounce of prevention"
so go to
www.clwbooks.com
RIGHT NOW
and purchase
extra copies
for your family
and friends.

If this book has enlightened
you or helped you prevent
being
involved in a scam,
please let us know.

Also, if you have any travel
stories you would like to
share we would love to hear
them,
just drop us a line at:

www.clwbooks.com

Made in the USA
San Bernardino, CA
06 November 2013